ANNY WINNY

A DAY IN ROME

Copyright © 2024 by Anny Winny

All rights reserved. No part of this publication may be reproduced, stored or transmitted in any form or by any means, electronic, mechanical, photocopying, recording, scanning, or otherwise without written permission from the publisher. It is illegal to copy this book, post it to a website, or distribute it by any other means without permission.

First edition

This book was professionally typeset on Reedsy.
Find out more at reedsy.com

This book is dedicated to God Almighty

Contents

Preface		ii
Acknowledgments		iv
1	Arrival in Rome	1
2	Breakfast with a View	5
3	A Stroll Through Trastevere	9
4	The Heart of Rome	13
5	A Night to Remember	17
6	Secrets of the Vatican	22
7	Twilight at Trastevere	27
8	A Hidden Gem	32
9	Unraveling the Past	37
10	A Glimpse of the Future	42
11	Echoes of the Past	47
12	A New Beginning	52
About the Author		57

Preface

A Day in Rome follows the transformative journey of Clara, a young woman seeking adventure and self-discovery in the enchanting city of Rome. Determined to escape her mundane routine, Clara embarks on a solo trip to Italy, hoping to immerse herself in the rich culture, history, and beauty of the Eternal City.

From the moment she arrives, Clara is captivated by Rome's charm, wandering through its iconic streets, historical landmarks, and vibrant neighborhoods. With her camera in hand, she explores the Colosseum, the Trevi Fountain, and the picturesque Trastevere district. Each location reveals not just the city's grandeur, but also a sense of freedom and joy she hasn't felt in years.

As she navigates through her adventure, Clara unexpectedly meets Gianni, a charismatic local who introduces her to the hidden gems of Rome. Their connection deepens as they share stories, laughter, and unforgettable experiences, including a romantic evening at the Colosseum under the stars. Gianni encourages Clara to embrace spontaneity, challenging her to let go of her past and embrace new beginnings.

Together, they traverse the city's winding streets, savor delicious gelato, and witness breathtaking views from Gianicolo Hill. With each shared moment, Clara discovers not only the beauty of Rome but also her own strength and desires. As the day unfolds, Clara confronts her fears and insecurities, realizing that this journey is not just about the sights she sees but also about the person she is becoming.

As Clara's trip comes to an end, she is faced with the prospect of leaving behind the newfound connection she has with Gianni. In a poignant moment atop Gianicolo Hill, they acknowledge their feelings for one another, setting the stage for a romantic possibility that transcends their brief encounter.

A Day in Rome is a heartfelt exploration of love, self-discovery, and the power of travel to change one's perspective. It illustrates how a single day in a foreign city can lead to profound personal growth and lasting connections, leaving Clara forever changed by her unforgettable experience in the Eternal City.

Acknowledgments

Thank you for your love and support

1

Arrival in Rome

The moment the plane touched down at Fiumicino Airport, Clara felt a rush of exhilaration. Rome, a city steeped in history and culture, had always been a dream destination for her. She could hardly believe she was finally here, ready to explore the cobblestone streets, ancient ruins, and vibrant piazzas that filled her imagination since childhood. As she disembarked, the scent of fresh espresso and pastries wafted through the air, beckoning her forward.

After clearing customs, Clara grabbed her suitcase and stepped out into the warm Roman sun. The air was thick with excitement and the melodic hum of Italian chatter. She spotted her taxi driver holding a sign with her name, and with a smile, she approached him. "Benvenuto a Roma!" he greeted, his eyes sparkling with enthusiasm. Clara returned his smile, her heart racing as she climbed into the backseat of the car.

The driver navigated the busy streets, and Clara gazed out the window, absorbing every sight. Ancient buildings with weathered facades stood next to modern shops, their vibrant colors clashing beautifully. The vibrant street life captivated her: couples strolled hand in hand, children laughed as they played, and vendors shouted about their wares. She could see the iconic red and yellow buildings of Rome in the distance, adorned with blooming bougainvillea that draped down like cascading jewels.

As they approached her hotel, a charming boutique establishment nestled on a quiet street near the heart of the city, Clara's anticipation grew. The driver expertly maneuvered the narrow streets, and soon they arrived at the hotel. Clara stepped out and was immediately struck by the quaint beauty of the building, its wrought-iron balconies adorned with pots of flowers.

Inside, the hotel was just as charming. The lobby was adorned with vintage decor, and the receptionist greeted her with a warm smile. "Welcome, Signorina Clara! We hope you enjoy your stay." After checking in and receiving her key, Clara made her way to her room.

The room was small but beautifully decorated with soft linens and antique furniture. She dropped her suitcase on the floor, took a deep breath, and stepped onto the balcony. Her breath caught as she gazed out at the stunning view. She could see the rooftops of Rome, the majestic dome of St. Peter's Basilica peeking through the buildings. The sun was beginning to set, casting a golden hue over the city, and Clara felt a sense of peace wash over her.

After refreshing herself, Clara decided to venture out. She pulled out her map, tracing her finger over the streets she had studied for months. Her first stop was the Colosseum, an ancient marvel she had longed to see. She stepped out of the hotel and joined the throngs of tourists, each one as eager as she was to experience the magic of Rome.

The streets were alive with the sounds of laughter and conversation. Clara followed the winding paths, stopping to admire a small gelato shop, its colorful offerings displayed like treasures. She couldn't resist and ordered a scoop of pistachio, savoring the creamy texture as she continued her journey.

As she neared the Colosseum, Clara could feel the weight of history pressing in around her. The massive structure loomed ahead, its weathered stones speaking of centuries of battles, crowds, and triumphs. She joined the line of eager tourists, her heart racing as she got closer. The moment she stepped through the archway and into the Colosseum, she was transported back in time.

Inside, the vast arena stretched out before her, and she could almost hear the roar of the crowd, the clash of swords, and the cries of the gladiators. Clara wandered through the ancient corridors, running her fingers along the cool stone walls. She closed her eyes for a moment, imagining the grandeur of the games that once captivated audiences from all walks of life.

"Excuse me, do you need a guide?" a voice interrupted her reverie. Clara turned to find a cheerful young man, his badge indicating he was a tour guide. "I can show you around and share some stories," he offered. Clara hesitated, then nodded, excited to learn more.

The guide led her through the Colosseum, sharing tales of its construction, the elaborate spectacles that took place, and the social dynamics of ancient Rome. Clara listened intently, captivated by the details. The guide's enthusiasm was infectious, and she found herself swept up in the drama of it all.

After the tour, Clara decided to take a moment to absorb the atmosphere. She found a quiet corner, sat down on a stone bench, and watched the sunset cast a warm glow over the Colosseum. People milled about, taking pictures, laughing, and sharing their own experiences. In that moment, Clara felt a profound connection to the city.

With her heart full and her mind buzzing with excitement, Clara knew this was just the beginning of her Roman adventure. As the sky darkened and the first stars appeared, she felt the thrill of anticipation for the discoveries that lay ahead.

Clara rose from the bench, dusted off her jeans, and headed back towards her hotel. She could hardly wait to see what tomorrow would bring in this beautiful, enchanting city. The streets were alive with energy as she walked back, filled with a sense of belonging and wonder. She had arrived in Rome, and the day was just the first chapter of her incredible journey.

2

Breakfast with a View

Clara woke up early the next morning, the golden rays of the sun filtering through her hotel room window and gently nudging her from sleep. She stretched and took a moment to absorb the warmth and serenity of the morning. Today was a new adventure, and her stomach growled in anticipation of a hearty Italian breakfast.

After freshening up, Clara slipped into a sundress, ideal for the warm Roman climate. She stepped out of her room and made her way to the hotel's rooftop terrace, which promised a spectacular view of the city. As she climbed the stairs, she could hear the distant sounds of the bustling streets below—the honking of cars, the laughter of tourists, and the melodic tones of Italian conversations.

When she reached the terrace, Clara was greeted by a stunning panorama. The rooftops of Rome spread out before her like a patchwork quilt, each building unique, yet all part of the beautiful tapestry of the city. She could see the majestic dome of St. Peter's Basilica in the distance, its silhouette highlighted against the clear blue sky. The sight took her breath away.

The aroma of fresh pastries and brewing coffee wafted through the air, guiding Clara to the breakfast spread. A friendly waiter welcomed her, gesturing toward an array of mouthwatering options: flaky croissants, cornetti (Italian croissants), and a selection of jams that sparkled like jewels. She selected a golden cornetto filled with rich chocolate, a slice of cake drizzled with honey, and a cappuccino that was frothy and inviting.

Carrying her tray to a cozy table near the edge of the terrace, Clara settled in, soaking in the view as she took her first sip of coffee. The rich, bold flavor danced on her palate, and she felt a wave of contentment wash over her. Each bite of the cornetto was a delightful indulgence, the chocolate melting in her mouth like a sweet embrace.

As she savored her breakfast, Clara noticed a couple sitting at the next table, animatedly discussing their plans for the day. They were speaking in rapid Italian, but Clara could pick up a few words here and there. The woman, with her flowing dress and sunhat, seemed to be passionately recounting a story, gesturing wildly with her hands. Clara couldn't help but smile; the vibrancy of the moment filled her with joy.

"Excuse me," Clara said, her curiosity getting the better of her. "What are you two planning to see today?"

The couple turned to her, their smiles warm and welcoming. "Ah, buongiorno!" the man replied, his accent thick and charming. "We are going to explore the Vatican and then visit the Sistine Chapel. Have you been?"

"I'm heading there today too!" Clara exclaimed, feeling a sense of camaraderie with them. They introduced themselves as Marco and Sofia, and they quickly struck up a friendly conversation.

As they exchanged travel stories, Marco and Sofia shared their favorite spots in Rome. "You must try the gelato at Giolitti," Marco insisted, his eyes sparkling with enthusiasm. "It's the best in the city!"

Sofia chimed in, "And don't forget to wander through the streets of Trastevere. It's like stepping into a postcard!" Clara made a mental note of their recommendations, grateful for the insider tips from the locals.

After finishing her breakfast, Clara lingered a moment longer, captivated by the view. She watched as the city began to come alive; people hustled to work, tourists snapped photos, and the gentle hum of life filled the air. It was a scene of perfect harmony, and Clara felt herself becoming part of it.

With a grateful smile and a wave goodbye to Marco and Sofia, Clara descended from the terrace and set off for the Vatican. She followed the winding streets, admiring the beautiful architecture around her. Each turn revealed another stunning building, adorned with intricate carvings and vibrant colors. The atmosphere was electric, and Clara felt invigorated by the lively spirit of the city.

As she approached St. Peter's Basilica, the massive dome towered above her, commanding attention and respect. Clara stood in awe, her heart racing with excitement. The basilica was even more breathtaking in person, its grandeur overwhelming. She joined the queue, the anticipation buzzing in the air as visitors from around the world shared their excitement.

Once inside, Clara was struck by the sheer beauty of the interior. The soaring ceilings, adorned with golden mosaics, seemed to touch the heavens. Sunlight streamed through the tall windows, illuminating the vast space and creating a sacred ambiance. Clara wandered through the aisles, her eyes wide with wonder. She felt a deep sense of reverence as she explored the artwork that surrounded her.

The highlight of her visit was, of course, the Sistine Chapel. As she entered, silence fell over the crowd, and Clara was immediately enveloped in the awe of Michelangelo's masterpiece. The ceiling, adorned with vibrant frescoes depicting biblical scenes, was a breathtaking spectacle. She stood in the center, gazing up, trying to absorb every detail. It was a moment of pure magic—a connection to the past that made her heart swell with gratitude.

After leaving the chapel, Clara felt a newfound sense of inspiration. The beauty and history of the Vatican had left an indelible mark on her soul. She took a deep breath, stepping out into the sunlight, ready to embrace the rest of her day in Rome.

Clara's mind buzzed with thoughts as she strolled through the Vatican gardens, the tranquility of the surroundings a refreshing contrast to the grandeur she had just witnessed. The lush greenery and fragrant flowers offered a moment of peace, allowing her to reflect on the beauty of her experiences so far.

As she exited the Vatican, Clara was eager to explore more of Rome. The streets beckoned her, filled with the promise of adventure, delicious food, and the chance to create unforgettable memories. She couldn't wait to uncover more hidden gems and experience the warmth of Roman hospitality. Today was just the beginning, and she felt a sense of exhilaration wash over her as she stepped back into the lively streets, ready for whatever lay ahead.

3

A Stroll Through Trastevere

With her heart still fluttering from the awe-inspiring visit to the Vatican, Clara set out to explore Trastevere, one of Rome's most enchanting neighborhoods. Known for its narrow cobblestone streets, charming squares, and vibrant atmosphere, Trastevere promised a delightful afternoon of discovery.

As she crossed the Tiber River via the picturesque Ponte Sisto, Clara felt the energy of the city shift. The bustling crowds and grand monuments faded, replaced by a more intimate and local ambiance. The air was filled with the enticing aroma of freshly baked bread and simmering sauces, a testament to the neighborhood's rich culinary scene. She took a deep breath, letting the smells guide her as she wandered deeper into Trastevere.

The first thing that struck Clara was the colorful architecture. The buildings, painted in soft hues of ochre, peach, and terracotta, seemed to glow under the midday sun. Flower boxes overflowed with vibrant blooms, and laundry hung between balconies, flapping gently in the warm breeze. It felt like a scene straight out of a painting, one that she wished she could capture forever.

Clara meandered through the winding streets, her senses alive with the sights and sounds around her. She passed small shops selling artisanal crafts, from hand-painted ceramics to intricate jewelry. She paused to admire a nearby shop filled with beautiful masks, their colors and designs captivating her imagination. Clara picked up a delicate mask adorned with gold and deep red, envisioning the stories it might tell during the Carnival season.

Continuing her exploration, Clara stumbled upon Piazza Santa Maria in Trastevere, a lively square bustling with locals and tourists alike. The centerpiece was the stunning Basilica di Santa Maria in Trastevere, its façade decorated with intricate mosaics that glimmered in the sunlight. Clara was drawn to the lively atmosphere, with musicians playing, children laughing, and people sitting at outdoor cafés, enjoying their meals.

Finding a shaded bench, Clara sat for a moment, watching the world go by. She felt a sense of belonging, as if she had been welcomed into the heart of the city. The sound of a guitar caught her attention, and she turned to see a young man performing a lively tune. His passion was infectious, and she couldn't help but tap her foot along with the rhythm.

After a while, Clara decided to join the crowd at a nearby café. The smell of espresso and fresh pastries lured her in, and she quickly found a table outside. She ordered a cappuccino and a slice of torta di ricotta, a creamy ricotta cake that had been recommended by the barista. As she savored each bite, Clara relished the moment, feeling as if she were experiencing life like a local.

Refreshed and invigorated, Clara continued her journey through Trastevere. She wandered into the narrow lanes, where each twist and turn revealed hidden treasures. She discovered small artisan shops, charming boutiques, and local markets brimming with fresh produce and handmade goods. She chatted with vendors, practicing her Italian and enjoying the warmth of their smiles.

One shop caught her eye—a quaint little store filled with handmade leather goods. The scent of rich leather enveloped her as she entered, and Clara was mesmerized by the craftsmanship on display. She picked up a soft leather wallet and a beautifully crafted handbag, imagining how perfect they would be as souvenirs of her trip. The shop owner, a friendly older woman, struck up a conversation with Clara, sharing stories of her family's business that had been passed down for generations.

Feeling inspired by the stories around her, Clara left the shop with her new treasures and continued her exploration. As the sun began to dip lower in the sky, casting a golden light over the streets, Clara stumbled upon the Orto Botanico, the Botanical Garden of Rome. The garden was a tranquil oasis, filled with lush greenery and vibrant flowers. Clara felt a sense of calm wash over her as she wandered through the pathways, admiring the various plants and trees.

Finding a quiet spot on a bench, she closed her eyes for a moment, listening to the gentle rustle of leaves and the distant sound of water flowing from a fountain. It was a moment of peace, a respite from the vibrant energy of the city. Clara felt grateful for the experiences she had already gathered, and she looked forward to what lay ahead.

After a leisurely stroll through the gardens, Clara headed toward the iconic Gianicolo Hill, eager to catch a glimpse of the stunning panoramic view of Rome. The ascent was steep but rewarding, and as she reached the top, she was greeted by one of the most breathtaking sights of her journey. The city sprawled out beneath her, a sea of terracotta roofs and majestic domes glowing in the soft evening light.

As she stood there, taking it all in, Clara felt a sense of connection to the city—a profound understanding that she was part of something larger than herself. The beauty of Rome was overwhelming, and she couldn't help but feel a surge of inspiration. This was a place where history, art, and life intertwined, creating a rich tapestry that she was only beginning to unravel.

As dusk fell, the city began to sparkle with lights, and Clara reluctantly turned to make her way back down. The streets were coming alive with a new energy, the chatter of voices and the clinking of glasses filling the air. Clara decided to join in on the evening festivities and found herself at a small trattoria, where the aroma of fresh pasta wafted through the open windows.

With a cheerful atmosphere surrounding her, Clara sat at a table outside, ready to indulge in a delicious dinner. She ordered a plate of cacio e pepe, a simple yet delectable dish of pasta, cheese, and pepper that was a staple of Roman cuisine. As she took her first bite, the flavors danced on her tongue, and she closed her eyes, savoring the rich and comforting taste.

After dinner, Clara took a leisurely stroll back through Trastevere, the streets aglow with twinkling lights. Musicians played in the squares, and laughter filled the air as people gathered to enjoy the lively atmosphere. Clara felt a sense of contentment as she absorbed the sights and sounds around her, grateful for the day's adventures and the connections she had made.

Finally, as she returned to her hotel, Clara reflected on the vibrant experiences of the day. From the awe of the Vatican to the charm of Trastevere, she felt truly alive in this incredible city. She knew that each day in Rome was a gift, filled with opportunities to explore, discover, and connect. With a heart full of joy and anticipation, Clara drifted off to sleep, dreaming of the adventures that awaited her in the days to come.

4

The Heart of Rome

The next morning, Clara awoke to the cheerful sound of birds chirping outside her window. She stretched lazily, feeling energized and eager for another day in the Eternal City. After quickly showering and dressing, she headed to the hotel's terrace for breakfast. Today, she opted for a traditional Italian breakfast of toast with olive oil and tomatoes, along with a rich espresso. She relished every bite, knowing that the day ahead promised more exciting adventures.

With her appetite satisfied, Clara set out to explore some of Rome's most iconic landmarks. Her first stop was the Colosseum, one of the most famous structures in the world. As she approached, the colossal arches and ancient stonework loomed before her, radiating history and grandeur. Clara felt a thrill of excitement as she joined the line of eager tourists waiting to enter.

Once inside, Clara marveled at the vastness of the arena, imagining the roaring crowds and fierce gladiators that once fought for their lives in this very place. She wandered through the ancient ruins, her fingers brushing against the cool stone walls as she envisioned the stories of triumph and defeat that echoed through the ages. An informative guidebook in hand, she read about the Colosseum's construction and its significance in ancient Rome, enriching her appreciation for the site.

After exploring the lower levels, Clara climbed to the upper tiers. The view from above was breathtaking, offering a panoramic perspective of the arena and the bustling city beyond. She took a moment to capture the scene with her camera, wanting to remember this moment forever. The juxtaposition of the ancient structure against the modern city was a reminder of how Rome beautifully blended the past with the present.

Next on her itinerary was the Roman Forum, located just a short walk away from the Colosseum. As Clara strolled through the ruins, she felt as though she had stepped back in time. The Forum was once the heart of ancient Rome, a place where citizens gathered for political, social, and religious events. Clara could see the remnants of temples, basilicas, and public spaces that had witnessed the rise and fall of empires.

As she wandered among the crumbling columns and uneven pathways, Clara imagined the vibrant life that once filled the Forum. She pictured merchants selling their goods, senators debating issues of the day, and citizens discussing news and gossip. The sense of history enveloped her, and she couldn't help but feel a profound connection to the past.

Finding a quiet spot on a stone bench overlooking the Forum, Clara took a moment to reflect. She pulled out her journal and began to write, capturing her thoughts and feelings about the incredible experiences she had had so far. Writing had always been a passion of hers, and it felt cathartic to document her journey through this remarkable city.

As she scribbled her thoughts, Clara noticed a small group of artists nearby, sketching the ruins with skillful precision. Inspired, she put her journal aside and pulled out her sketchbook. With a few strokes of her pencil, she began to capture the essence of the Forum, the delicate lines reflecting her interpretation of the beauty before her. Time seemed to fade away as she lost herself in the rhythm of drawing, each line bringing her closer to the spirit of Rome.

Eventually, Clara felt a gentle tap on her shoulder. Startled, she turned to find an elderly gentleman watching her, a warm smile on his face. "You have a gift," he said, his Italian accent thick yet friendly. "Your drawing captures the soul of this place."

Clara blushed, feeling a mix of shyness and pride. "Thank you! I just wanted to capture the beauty of the Forum."

The man nodded appreciatively. "It is important to remember what we see, to hold onto these moments. My name is Gianni, and I am a painter. Would you like to see my work?"

Curious and excited, Clara agreed, and Gianni led her to a nearby art studio that he owned. The studio was filled with vibrant paintings of Rome—its streets, people, and landscapes. Each piece told a story, capturing the essence of the city through Gianni's eyes.

As they walked through the gallery, Clara was struck by Gianni's passion for his craft. He spoke animatedly about each painting, sharing anecdotes about his experiences as an artist in Rome. Clara felt a connection to him, as if they were kindred spirits united by their love of art and creativity.

"Every artist sees Rome differently," Gianni said, his eyes twinkling. "We each have a unique perspective, and that is what makes our art so special."

Inspired by Gianni's words, Clara felt invigorated. She expressed her desire to explore more of Rome's art scene and to create more of her own work during her stay. Gianni offered to show her around some hidden galleries and studios later that week, and Clara happily accepted.

After their visit, Clara left the studio feeling inspired and excited about the artistic possibilities that lay ahead. She continued her exploration of the Forum, taking in the beauty around her with fresh eyes. The experience with Gianni ignited her passion for art, reminding her of the importance of following her creative instincts.

As the sun began to lower in the sky, Clara made her way to her next destination—the Pantheon. The majestic structure had been on her list since she arrived in Rome, and she couldn't wait to see it up close. As she approached, the imposing columns of the Pantheon stood proudly against the sky, and Clara felt a sense of awe wash over her.

Stepping inside, she was struck by the breathtaking dome overhead, with its oculus allowing natural light to pour in. The space felt sacred, and Clara could feel the weight of history within its walls. She wandered through the interior, admiring the beautiful sculptures and tombs, including that of the artist Raphael.

As she left the Pantheon, Clara felt a deep appreciation for the artistry and architecture that defined Rome. The city was a living museum, filled with treasures waiting to be discovered. She made her way to a nearby gelateria, craving a sweet treat after her busy day.

Settling on a bench with a scoop of pistachio gelato, Clara watched as the sun set over Rome, painting the sky with hues of pink and orange. She felt a sense of peace and fulfillment wash over her, grateful for the incredible experiences she had shared with the city and its people. With her heart full and her mind racing with ideas, Clara couldn't wait to see what adventures awaited her in the days to come.

As she savored her gelato, she made a promise to herself: to embrace each moment, to capture the beauty of Rome through her art and words, and to continue exploring the vibrant tapestry of life that surrounded her. With that resolve, Clara rose from the bench, ready to embrace whatever the night had in store.

5

A Night to Remember

As the sun dipped below the horizon, Clara felt a renewed sense of excitement for the evening ahead. She had read about the vibrant nightlife in Rome, a city that transformed after dark, bursting with energy, laughter, and music. Tonight, she planned to meet up with Gianni for dinner, and she was eager to learn more about the local culture through his eyes.

Clara returned to her hotel to freshen up, slipping into a light sundress that she hoped would capture the essence of Roman summer nights. The streets below her window were already alive with the sounds of clinking glasses and soft chatter as restaurants prepared for the dinner rush. She applied a touch of makeup, excited for the adventure that awaited her.

Meeting Gianni at a quaint trattoria nestled in a cobblestone alley, Clara was greeted with a warm hug. "You look beautiful!" he exclaimed, gesturing for her to take a seat at a small table outside, adorned with flickering candles. The atmosphere was enchanting, with fairy lights strung above, illuminating the lively crowd around them.

"Thank you, Gianni! This place is wonderful," Clara said, taking in her surroundings. The scent of garlic and fresh basil wafted through the air, making her stomach rumble in anticipation.

As they perused the menu, Gianni shared stories of his favorite dishes, explaining the significance of each one in Roman culture. Clara decided on cacio e pepe, a simple yet delicious pasta dish made with Pecorino Romano cheese and black pepper, while Gianni chose saltimbocca alla Romana, a classic Roman dish featuring veal topped with prosciutto and sage.

When their food arrived, Clara took a moment to appreciate the presentation before digging in. The first bite of her pasta was heavenly—the creamy texture combined with the sharpness of the cheese danced on her taste buds. "This is incredible! I think I've died and gone to heaven," she exclaimed, savoring the flavors.

Gianni chuckled, enjoying her enthusiasm. "Rome has a way of enchanting everyone, especially through its food. Each bite tells a story of tradition and passion."

They continued to enjoy their meal, sharing laughter and anecdotes about their lives, their dreams, and their love for art. Gianni spoke fondly of the artists who had walked the streets of Rome before him—Titian, Caravaggio, and Michelangelo. Clara was captivated by his knowledge and passion for the arts. She found herself imagining the world of art in Italy, the profound influence it had on the global stage.

After finishing their meal, Clara and Gianni decided to take a stroll through the streets of Trastevere, one of Rome's most charming neighborhoods. The narrow, winding alleys were filled with vibrant murals, quaint shops, and lively piazzas. As they walked, the sounds of street performers filled the air—musicians playing traditional Italian songs and artists showcasing their talents to captivated audiences.

Clara spotted a small group of people gathered around a street musician strumming a guitar. She could feel the infectious energy in the air as onlookers sang along. Drawn in by the music, she and Gianni stopped to enjoy the performance. The artist's voice was smooth and melodic, evoking a sense of nostalgia that stirred something deep within Clara.

As the final note faded, Clara clapped enthusiastically, feeling a rush of joy. Gianni turned to her with a grin. "Would you like to join me for a dance?"

Clara's heart raced at the suggestion. She had never considered herself a dancer, but the atmosphere was irresistible. "Why not?" she replied with a playful smile, taking his hand as they moved to the side of the gathering.

With the music still playing softly in the background, they began to sway to the rhythm, Clara letting loose and allowing herself to be swept away by the moment. Laughter erupted between them as they twirled and spun, and Clara felt a sense of freedom she hadn't experienced in a long time.

After a few minutes, they stepped back, breathless and grinning from ear to ear. "That was so much fun!" Clara exclaimed, still catching her breath. "I didn't think I could dance like that."

Gianni chuckled, "In Rome, anything is possible. The city has a magic about it that brings out the best in people."

As they continued their stroll through Trastevere, Clara noticed the vibrant energy of the neighborhood. People were sitting outside cafes, sipping wine, and engaging in animated conversations. The air was thick with the sounds of laughter and clinking glasses, creating a festive atmosphere that felt intoxicating.

They stumbled upon a small piazza where a local festival was taking place. Colorful lights adorned the trees, and stalls offered delicious treats and handmade crafts. Clara's eyes sparkled with excitement. "Let's check it out!" she suggested, pulling Gianni toward a stand filled with fresh cannoli.

"Excellent choice," he replied, his eyes twinkling. "You must try the cannoli. They are the best in the city."

As Clara bit into the crispy shell filled with sweet ricotta, she closed her eyes in delight. The combination of textures and flavors was heavenly. "This is amazing! I can't believe I've been missing out on this," she exclaimed, savoring every bite.

After indulging in the cannoli, they meandered through the stalls, stopping to admire handcrafted jewelry, paintings, and local crafts. Clara found herself drawn to a painting that captured the essence of a Roman sunset. The warm hues of orange and pink mirrored the colors of the sky that evening. She felt a strong connection to the piece, and before she knew it, she was pulling out her wallet to make the purchase.

"Art has a way of capturing moments," Gianni observed as Clara handed over the cash. "It's like carrying a piece of a memory with you."

As the night wore on, Clara and Gianni shared stories with the vendors and other festival-goers, creating an atmosphere of camaraderie and joy. They danced to live music, joined in the laughter, and made new friends under the starlit sky.

As the festival began to wind down, Clara felt a sense of gratitude wash over her. The connections she had made, the experiences she had shared, and the beauty of the city were all woven into a tapestry of unforgettable memories.

"Thank you for tonight, Gianni. I never imagined my time in Rome would be so magical," Clara said as they walked back toward the river, the shimmering water reflecting the glow of the moon.

"It's just the beginning, Clara. There's so much more to discover," he replied, his voice filled with warmth.

As they strolled alongside the Tiber River, Clara felt a sense of belonging. The city had embraced her in a way she had never expected. She was falling in love with Rome—its history, its art, and its people. With each step, she realized that this journey was not just about the sights she would see but the connections she would forge and the stories she would create along the way.

With her heart full of hope and excitement, Clara looked forward to what the next day would bring, knowing that in a city like Rome, every moment had the potential to become a cherished memory.

6

Secrets of the Vatican

The next morning, Clara awoke with a sense of anticipation coursing through her veins. Today was the day she would explore the Vatican, a place she had long dreamed of visiting. The mere thought of stepping into such a significant historical and spiritual center filled her with awe.

After a quick breakfast at her hotel, Clara donned a modest dress, mindful of the Vatican's dress code. She had heard that visitors were expected to dress conservatively, with shoulders and knees covered. Grabbing her camera, she made her way to the Vatican, excitement bubbling within her.

As she approached the entrance, Clara was struck by the sheer scale of St. Peter's Basilica. The grand façade loomed above her, adorned with intricate sculptures and detailed artwork. She stood in line, surrounded by tourists from all over the world, their languages a chorus of excitement and wonder.

Once inside, Clara felt a profound sense of reverence. The vastness of the basilica took her breath away. Sunlight streamed through the massive windows, illuminating the interior and creating a warm, golden glow. Every detail was a testament to the artistry and devotion that had gone into the construction of this sacred space.

Clara wandered through the basilica, her eyes wide as she admired Michelangelo's Pietà, the stunning marble sculpture of Mary holding the body of Jesus. The emotion captured in the figures resonated deeply with her, and she felt tears prick her eyes. She stood silently for a moment, absorbing the beauty and sorrow of the piece before moving on.

Next, she made her way to the tomb of St. Peter, whose legacy had shaped the very foundation of the Catholic Church. Clara knelt for a brief moment of reflection, offering her own thoughts and prayers. It felt surreal to be in a place so rich with history, where countless souls had come to seek solace and guidance.

After exploring the basilica, Clara joined a guided tour of the Vatican Museums. She was eager to learn about the treasures housed within these walls. As they moved through the corridors, Clara listened intently as the guide spoke about the vast collection of art and artifacts, each piece telling a story of its own.

The Raphael Rooms captivated Clara. The vivid colors and intricate details of the frescoes transported her to another time. She marveled at "The School of Athens," where philosophers from different eras gathered in a harmonious dialogue. The scene was a celebration of knowledge and enlightenment, and Clara felt inspired by the message of unity it conveyed.

As they continued, Clara's heart raced at the thought of entering the Sistine Chapel. She had always dreamed of seeing Michelangelo's iconic ceiling, and now she was just moments away. The anticipation grew, and she could hardly contain her excitement.

Finally, they entered the chapel, and Clara's breath caught in her throat. The room was awe-inspiring, adorned with vibrant colors and intricate details that seemed to come alive. She looked up at the ceiling, her eyes widening in disbelief as she took in the magnificence of "The Creation of Adam." The depiction of God and Adam reaching out to one another transcended time, a powerful representation of humanity's connection to the divine.

Clara felt a wave of emotion wash over her. In that moment, surrounded by the beauty and history of the chapel, she understood the significance of this place. It was not just a tourist destination but a sacred space that had inspired countless people throughout history.

As she stood there, lost in thought, Clara noticed Gianni entering the chapel. He scanned the room until his eyes met hers, and a warm smile spread across his face. After the tour, he approached her, and they stepped outside, their eyes still sparkling from the wonders they had just witnessed.

"How was it?" Gianni asked, his voice filled with enthusiasm.

Clara could hardly find the words to express her feelings. "It was beyond anything I imagined. The art, the history—it's all so profound," she replied, her voice barely above a whisper.

"I'm glad you enjoyed it," he said, taking her hand and leading her toward a small café nearby. "Let's grab a coffee and talk about it."

Settling at a table outside the café, they ordered espressos and pastries, eager to share their thoughts. Clara recounted her favorite moments from the tour, and Gianni listened intently, nodding along as she spoke.

"I've always believed that art can connect people on a deeper level," Gianni remarked. "It's a language that transcends words."

Clara smiled, appreciating his insight. "You're right. I felt so moved by everything I saw today. It's like each piece has a heartbeat."

As they sipped their coffees, Clara noticed the lively atmosphere of the streets around them. Artists painted on easels, musicians played softly in the background, and the aroma of fresh food wafted through the air. She felt the heartbeat of Rome in that moment—a vibrant blend of culture, history, and creativity.

After finishing their coffees, Clara and Gianni decided to stroll through the nearby gardens of Vatican City. The lush greenery and blooming flowers offered a serene escape from the crowds, and they enjoyed the tranquility of the space.

"Have you ever thought about what it means to create?" Gianni asked as they walked along a shaded path. "To share a part of yourself with the world?"

Clara pondered his question, appreciating the depth of his thoughts. "I think creating is about vulnerability. It's about sharing your experiences and emotions, hoping someone else can connect with them."

"Exactly," Gianni replied, his eyes shining with enthusiasm. "That's the beauty of art—it's a reflection of our humanity."

As they wandered through the gardens, they stumbled upon a small fountain surrounded by benches. Clara took a seat, and Gianni joined her. The sound of water flowing created a soothing backdrop as they continued their conversation.

"Do you paint or create art yourself?" Clara asked, curious about Gianni's artistic inclinations.

"I dabble in photography," he confessed, pulling out his camera. "I love capturing moments and emotions through the lens. It allows me to tell stories in a unique way."

Clara's eyes lit up at the mention of photography. "That's incredible! I'd love to see some of your work."

Gianni smiled, scrolling through his camera's gallery. "Here, let me show you." He turned the screen toward her, revealing stunning images of Rome—the vibrant streets, the intricate architecture, and candid moments of people lost in their own worlds.

"This is beautiful!" Clara exclaimed, captivated by his eye for detail. "You have a talent for capturing the essence of the city."

"Thank you," Gianni replied, a hint of pride in his voice. "I love showing others the beauty I see through my lens."

As they shared more of their artistic passions, Clara felt a deeper connection forming between them. Gianni's insights and enthusiasm mirrored her own, creating a bond that felt both genuine and exhilarating.

After a while, Clara checked her watch and realized it was time to head back. "I have a reservation at a local restaurant tonight," she said, reluctance creeping into her voice. "I wish we could continue exploring."

"Let's make a plan to meet up again soon," Gianni suggested, his eyes bright with anticipation. "There's so much more of Rome to see together."

Clara nodded, grateful for the connection they had forged during their time together. "I'd love that."

As they walked back toward the entrance of Vatican City, Clara took one last look at the stunning architecture, her heart full of gratitude for the experiences she had gained that day. The secrets of the Vatican had revealed not just art and history, but a deeper understanding of herself and her place in the world.

With a promise to meet again, Clara waved goodbye to Gianni and stepped into the bustling streets of Rome, ready to embrace whatever the rest of her day would bring.

7

Twilight at Trastevere

As the sun began to dip below the horizon, casting a warm golden hue over the city, Clara found herself wandering through the charming streets of Trastevere. This neighborhood, known for its narrow cobblestone lanes and vibrant atmosphere, beckoned her with its promise of authentic Roman culture. The air was filled with the rich aroma of Italian cuisine, and she could hear the distant laughter of families gathering for dinner.

Clara had heard stories about Trastevere's enchanting ambiance and lively nightlife, and she was eager to experience it for herself. She strolled past colorful buildings adorned with ivy, their balconies bursting with flowers, and felt an overwhelming sense of warmth and hospitality. The atmosphere was alive, and she could sense the pulse of the city in the air.

As she walked, Clara spotted a small pizzeria that looked inviting. The rustic wooden sign above the door read "Da Enzo al 29." The sound of laughter and clinking glasses spilled out, drawing her in. It seemed like the perfect place to indulge in some authentic Roman pizza.

Inside, the cozy interior was filled with laughter and the savory scent of freshly baked pizzas. Clara was greeted by a friendly waitress who led her to a small table by the window. She settled in, glancing at the menu, her mouth watering at the thought of trying the famous Margherita pizza.

While waiting for her meal, Clara took a moment to soak in the ambiance. The walls were adorned with photos of happy customers and vibrant paintings, each telling a story of shared meals and cherished memories. She felt a sense of belonging in this lively space, even as a solo traveler.

When her pizza arrived, Clara's eyes widened at the sight. The crust was golden and crispy, topped with vibrant red tomatoes, creamy mozzarella, and fragrant basil. She took her first bite, and a wave of delight washed over her. The flavors danced on her palate, each ingredient fresh and perfectly balanced.

As she savored her meal, Clara couldn't help but notice the animated conversations happening around her. Families and friends laughed and shared stories, their voices creating a beautiful symphony of connection. In that moment, she felt a pang of nostalgia for her own family, who she missed dearly. Yet, the joy of the people around her reminded her of the importance of connection, even in moments of solitude.

After finishing her pizza, Clara decided to explore the streets of Trastevere further. She wandered aimlessly, her heart light as she immersed herself in the vibrant culture around her. The streets were adorned with twinkling lights, and musicians played soft melodies on street corners, adding to the enchanting atmosphere.

As she turned a corner, Clara stumbled upon the beautiful Santa Maria in Trastevere, a stunning basilica that glowed in the soft evening light. The intricate mosaics above the entrance depicted scenes from the life of the Virgin Mary, their colors shimmering like jewels. Clara felt drawn to the basilica, and she stepped inside, captivated by the serene ambiance.

Inside, the hushed whispers of visitors mingled with the soft flickering of candles, creating an atmosphere of reverence. Clara took a moment to admire the grandeur of the interior, with its gilded ceilings and ornate altars. She found a quiet corner to sit and reflect, feeling grateful for the experiences she had accumulated on her journey.

Just as she was lost in thought, her phone buzzed, breaking the peaceful silence. It was a message from Gianni: "Hey! I hope you're enjoying Trastevere. Would you like to meet up for gelato? There's a place I think you'll love!"

A smile spread across Clara's face at the thought of seeing Gianni again. She quickly replied, agreeing to meet at the gelato shop he suggested. After a few more moments of contemplation in the basilica, she stepped back out into the lively streets.

Following Gianni's directions, Clara made her way to "Gelateria dei Gracchi," a local favorite known for its artisanal gelato. The line stretched out the door, a testament to its popularity. As she waited, Clara's anticipation grew. She scanned the menu, already dreaming of which flavors she would try.

Moments later, Gianni arrived, his face lighting up when he saw her. "Clara! I'm glad you could make it!" he exclaimed, pulling her into a warm embrace. The energy between them felt electric, and Clara's heart raced.

"I couldn't resist the idea of gelato," she replied, her smile mirroring his excitement.

They joined the line together, their conversation flowing effortlessly as they shared their favorite experiences from the day. Clara recounted her visit to the Vatican, and Gianni shared stories from his own explorations in Rome. They exchanged laughter and playful banter, creating a sense of camaraderie that felt both comforting and exhilarating.

When it was finally their turn, Clara eagerly approached the counter, greeted by a dazzling array of flavors. "What do you recommend?" she asked the gelato maker, her eyes wide with wonder.

"Try the pistachio and stracciatella," he suggested with a smile. "They're our specialties!"

Clara followed his recommendation, and Gianni opted for dark chocolate and hazelnut. They stepped outside with their cones, the cool evening breeze refreshing against their skin.

As they walked along the cobblestone streets, Clara savored each bite of her gelato, the creamy texture melting in her mouth. The flavors were intense and authentic, a perfect indulgence after her earlier meal.

"Isn't it amazing how something as simple as gelato can bring people together?" Gianni remarked, his gaze fixed on her with genuine warmth.

Clara nodded, feeling the truth in his words. "It's like a celebration of life's small pleasures," she said, glancing at the bustling streets filled with laughter and joy.

They continued their stroll through Trastevere, stopping occasionally to take pictures and admire the vibrant street art that adorned the walls. The atmosphere was alive with music and laughter, a perfect reflection of the city's spirit.

As they turned a corner, they found themselves in Piazza Trilussa, where a group of street performers captivated a crowd with their lively music. Clara and Gianni joined the spectators, swaying to the rhythm of the lively tunes. The energy was infectious, and Clara felt herself getting lost in the moment, her heart dancing along with the music.

When the performance ended, the crowd erupted in applause, and Clara turned to Gianni, her eyes shining with excitement. "This city is incredible! I'm so glad we're experiencing it together."

"Me too," Gianni replied, his expression softening as he looked at her. "I've really enjoyed getting to know you, Clara."

Their eyes met for a moment, and Clara felt a flutter in her chest. She couldn't deny the chemistry that had developed between them throughout their time together.

As the night wore on, Clara knew this day in Rome was a chapter she would cherish forever. With Gianni by her side, she felt a sense of adventure and connection, discovering not just the beauty of the city but also the beauty of shared experiences. As they wandered the enchanting streets, Clara realized that sometimes the best moments were those spent with newfound friends, and she was grateful for every second spent in the vibrant heart of Trastevere.

8

A Hidden Gem

The sun rose the next morning, casting a soft light over Rome, signaling the start of a new day filled with possibilities. Clara woke up in her cozy apartment, still buzzing from the excitement of the previous night. The laughter, the gelato, and the warmth of Gianni's company lingered in her mind as she got ready for the day. After a quick breakfast of fresh bread and a strong Italian coffee, she set out to explore more of the city.

Her plan for the day was to visit the lesser-known spots in Rome, places that often escaped the typical tourist's eye. She had read about a few hidden gems, and her sense of adventure urged her to discover them. Armed with her camera and a small notebook, she headed towards the neighborhood of Testaccio, known for its authentic Roman food and local culture.

As Clara strolled through the streets of Testaccio, she was struck by the local charm. The area was less crowded than the city center, with quaint shops lining the streets and locals going about their daily routines. The lively market, Mercato di Testaccio, was bustling with vendors selling fresh produce, cheeses, and various culinary delights. The vivid colors of the fruits and vegetables, combined with the inviting aromas wafting from the food stalls, drew her in.

She decided to explore the market, wandering through the stalls and soaking in the vibrant atmosphere. Clara stopped at a stand selling ripe tomatoes and basil, admiring the quality of the produce. The vendor, an elderly man with a warm smile, noticed her interest. "These tomatoes are the best in Rome! Perfect for a caprese salad," he said, gesturing proudly to his display.

Clara smiled back, feeling a wave of connection with the vendor. "I can imagine! They look amazing," she replied, her enthusiasm genuine. She chatted with him for a few minutes, learning about his family's long history of farming in the region. His passion for fresh, local ingredients resonated with her, and she made a mental note to try cooking with these tomatoes during her stay.

Continuing through the market, Clara stumbled upon a small bakery. The scent of freshly baked bread was irresistible, and she couldn't help but go inside. The walls were lined with golden loaves, pastries, and traditional Roman sweets. She ordered a cornetto, a flaky pastry filled with cream, and enjoyed it at a small table while sipping on a cappuccino. The combination was divine, and Clara savored each bite, feeling as if she was truly experiencing the heart of Roman culinary culture.

After her delightful breakfast, Clara ventured to the nearby Cimitero Acattolico, or the Non-Catholic Cemetery. Tucked away from the hustle and bustle, this peaceful resting place was known for its beautiful greenery and the famous figures buried there, including the English poet John Keats. Clara felt drawn to this serene spot, eager to escape the crowds and immerse herself in the tranquility it offered.

As she entered the cemetery, Clara was greeted by the sight of lush trees, delicate flowers, and beautifully crafted tombstones. The atmosphere was serene, and she found a quiet path to wander. She admired the intricate sculptures and the care that had been taken to maintain the graves. The sound of birds chirping and the rustle of leaves created a perfect backdrop for reflection.

Clara soon found the grave of John Keats, marked by a simple stone with an inscription that spoke of his love for beauty and his longing for peace. Kneeling before the grave, she felt a connection to the poet, his words echoing in her mind. Inspired by his life and legacy, she took out her notebook and began to jot down her thoughts, allowing her emotions to flow freely onto the pages. Writing amidst such beauty felt sacred, and she found herself pouring her heart into her words.

After spending time in the cemetery, Clara emerged feeling renewed and inspired. She decided to explore the nearby Aventine Hill, known for its stunning views of the city and the famous keyhole view at the Knights of Malta. As she climbed the hill, she marveled at the charming gardens and quiet streets, feeling the weight of the city fade away with each step.

When she reached the top, she approached the iconic keyhole. Peering through the small hole, Clara gasped in amazement. The view was breathtaking: a perfectly framed glimpse of St. Peter's Basilica, the dome glowing in the afternoon light, surrounded by vibrant greenery. She took a moment to appreciate the scene, capturing it with her camera to remember the magic of that moment.

Feeling invigorated, Clara wandered into the Giardino degli Aranci, a beautiful orange garden that offered panoramic views of Rome. The garden was filled with sweet-smelling orange trees and peaceful benches, perfect for taking in the scenery. Clara found a spot to sit and reflect, enjoying the gentle breeze as she looked out over the city. The rooftops, ancient ruins, and bustling streets created a tapestry that spoke to the rich history of Rome.

As she sat, her thoughts drifted back to Gianni. She wondered what he was doing at that moment and if he would be interested in joining her on her adventures later that day. Clara decided to send him a message, suggesting they meet up for lunch at a local trattoria she had heard about during her exploration.

Once she had sent the message, she wandered through the garden, admiring the flowers and the peaceful atmosphere. The sun continued its descent, casting a warm glow on everything it touched. After a while, Clara's phone buzzed. Gianni had replied, and she couldn't help but smile at his enthusiasm: "I'd love to! Can't wait to hear about your adventures!"

Feeling a sense of excitement, Clara made her way down the hill toward the trattoria. She found it nestled among the charming streets, its outdoor seating filled with locals enjoying their meals. She stepped inside and found a cozy table by the window, eagerly anticipating Gianni's arrival.

As she waited, Clara took in her surroundings. The walls were adorned with photos of famous patrons and handwritten menus showcasing the day's specials. The air was filled with the comforting aroma of simmering sauces and freshly baked bread, making her stomach rumble with anticipation.

Soon, Gianni arrived, a smile lighting up his face as he spotted Clara. "Hey! Sorry I'm late; I got caught up with a few things," he said as he took a seat across from her.

"No worries! I've just been soaking in the atmosphere. This place is amazing!" Clara replied, her excitement contagious.

They perused the menu together, exchanging recommendations and laughter as they navigated the Italian dishes. Clara opted for cacio e pepe, a simple yet delicious pasta dish, while Gianni chose the saltimbocca, thin slices of veal wrapped in prosciutto.

As they waited for their meals, the conversation flowed effortlessly. Clara shared her experiences from the morning, her eyes lighting up as she described the charm of Testaccio and the tranquility of the cemetery. Gianni listened intently, his own experiences adding to the tapestry of their shared adventure.

When their food arrived, Clara's mouth watered at the sight. Each dish was beautifully presented, and the flavors were even better than she had imagined. They clinked their glasses of wine, toasting to friendship and new experiences.

"This is delicious! I'm so glad we decided to meet up," Clara said, savoring the first bite of her pasta.

"Me too! It's great to share these moments with someone who appreciates them," Gianni replied, his eyes sparkling with enthusiasm.

As they finished their meal, Clara felt a sense of contentment wash over her. The day had unfolded beautifully, filled with discovery, inspiration, and the blossoming friendship with Gianni. Little did she know that the adventures they were about to embark on together would lead to even deeper connections and unforgettable memories, intertwining their lives in ways she could never have imagined.

9

Unraveling the Past

The next morning, Clara woke with the dawn, the golden sunlight filtering through the curtains of her apartment. She felt invigorated and eager to continue her exploration of Rome. Today, she had a specific destination in mind: the Capitoline Museums. She had read about their vast collection of art and antiquities, and she couldn't wait to immerse herself in the history that filled those walls.

After a quick breakfast of toast and fresh fruit, Clara gathered her belongings, including her camera and notebook, and set out for the museums. The streets were quieter than usual, with a light morning breeze carrying the scents of freshly baked bread and coffee. As she walked, she took in the beauty of the city, from the charming balconies adorned with flowers to the sound of distant laughter echoing in the alleys.

Arriving at the Capitoline Museums, Clara was struck by the grandeur of the entrance. The massive marble stairs led up to an impressive façade, and she felt a thrill of excitement as she stepped inside. The museums were a treasure trove of artifacts and art, showcasing the rich history of Rome from ancient times to the Renaissance.

As she wandered through the halls, Clara found herself captivated by the sculptures, paintings, and mosaics. She marveled at the famous statue of Marcus Aurelius, his stoic expression and regal presence commanding attention. Clara spent hours exploring the various exhibits, jotting down her thoughts and impressions in her notebook, capturing the essence of the art and history surrounding her.

In one of the galleries, Clara discovered a section dedicated to ancient Roman life. The artifacts on display—ceramics, tools, and household items—provided a glimpse into the daily lives of Romans centuries ago. She found herself imagining what life must have been like, drawing parallels between their experiences and her own.

As she continued to explore, Clara's gaze fell upon a beautifully preserved fresco depicting a lavish banquet. The vibrant colors and intricate details transported her to another time. She could almost hear the laughter and chatter of guests, the clinking of goblets, and the music playing in the background. Inspired, she pulled out her notebook and began to sketch the scene, capturing the joy and festivity of the moment.

Hours passed as Clara lost herself in the art, but she eventually felt the pangs of hunger reminding her it was time to break for lunch. Stepping outside, she decided to explore the nearby area, hoping to find a cozy café where she could enjoy a meal.

Wandering the streets, Clara stumbled upon a small, family-owned trattoria that exuded warmth and authenticity. The wooden tables were filled with locals enjoying their meals, and the aroma of garlic and herbs wafted through the air. It felt like the perfect place to take a break and recharge.

After ordering a plate of pasta with a rich tomato sauce, Clara settled into a corner table. As she waited for her food, she reflected on her time in the museums and the stories the artifacts told. Each piece was a reminder of the intricate tapestry of history that had shaped Rome, and she felt grateful for the opportunity to experience it firsthand.

Just as her meal arrived, Clara's phone buzzed with a message from Gianni. "Hey! Hope you're having a great day! Want to meet up later? There's a cool event at the Piazza Navona tonight."

Clara smiled, thrilled at the prospect of spending more time with him. She quickly replied, "Absolutely! What time should we meet?"

After a few moments, Gianni responded, suggesting they meet at 6 PM. Clara finished her meal and made her way back to her apartment, feeling excited about the evening ahead. She had enjoyed her day of exploration, but the thought of sharing new experiences with Gianni filled her with anticipation.

Back at her apartment, Clara took some time to freshen up. She chose a simple yet elegant dress, one that she felt comfortable and confident in. After applying a touch of makeup and curling her hair, she glanced at the mirror, feeling ready for the night ahead.

As the clock approached 6 PM, Clara headed out, her heart racing with excitement. The streets were alive with energy, and the sun began to set, casting a warm glow over the city. When she arrived at Piazza Navona, the atmosphere was vibrant and festive. Street performers entertained crowds, artists displayed their work, and the sounds of laughter and music filled the air.

Spotting Gianni near the fountain, Clara felt her heart skip a beat. He looked handsome in a crisp shirt and jeans, his smile radiant as he waved her over. "You look amazing!" he said, his eyes sparkling with admiration.

"Thanks! This place is incredible," Clara replied, her own excitement bubbling over.

They wandered through the piazza, taking in the sights and sounds. Clara admired the magnificent fountains, particularly Bernini's Fontana dei Quattro Fiumi, with its grand statues and intricate details. Gianni shared stories about the piazza's history, explaining how it had once been a marketplace and a center of social life in Rome.

As the evening progressed, they stumbled upon a local artisan fair taking place in the square. Handcrafted jewelry, paintings, and pottery filled the stalls, each item telling its own story. Clara felt drawn to a booth selling handmade ceramics, their colors vibrant and patterns unique. She picked up a small bowl, admiring the craftsmanship, and decided to buy it as a souvenir.

Gianni, noticing her interest, encouraged her to negotiate with the seller. "It's part of the experience! You can get a better deal," he said with a grin. Clara hesitated but soon found herself engaged in a playful back-and-forth with the vendor, finally securing a small discount.

"See? You're a natural!" Gianni laughed, and Clara felt a rush of pride.

With her new treasure in hand, they continued to explore the fair, sampling local delicacies and chatting with the artisans. The energy of the piazza was contagious, and Clara felt as though she was part of something special—a living tapestry of culture and creativity.

As night fell, the piazza transformed into a magical scene illuminated by twinkling lights. Clara and Gianni found a spot at a café overlooking the fountain, ordering a bottle of wine to share. The ambiance was perfect, with the sound of laughter and music filling the air.

"Tonight feels like a dream," Clara said, gazing out at the beauty of the square. "I never imagined I would experience something like this in Rome."

Gianni raised his glass. "To new adventures and unforgettable moments," he said, his voice warm and inviting.

They clinked their glasses, the sound resonating with the joy of the evening. As they sipped their wine, the conversation flowed freely, ranging from their dreams and aspirations to their favorite travel experiences. Clara felt a connection with Gianni growing deeper, the laughter and shared stories weaving an invisible bond between them.

As the night progressed, they walked along the cobblestone streets, the glow of street lamps casting a soft light on their path. Clara felt a sense of belonging in the city, a feeling that had been missing for a long time. With Gianni by her side, she felt safe and exhilarated, ready to embrace whatever adventures awaited them in the days to come.

Unbeknownst to Clara, this night would be just the beginning of a journey that would unravel more than just the history of Rome; it would unravel her own heart and lead her to unexpected places she had never dared to dream of.

10

A Glimpse of the Future

The following morning, Clara awoke to the sound of soft rain tapping against her window. It was a stark contrast to the vibrant night she had experienced at Piazza Navona. As she pulled back the curtains, she watched droplets race down the glass, each one carving a path that reminded her of the unpredictable journey she was on. Despite the dreary weather, Clara felt a spark of excitement.

Today was Sunday, and she had plans to explore the Vatican City. The thought of standing beneath the majestic dome of St. Peter's Basilica filled her with anticipation. After quickly showering and getting dressed, Clara grabbed her raincoat and headed out, determined to make the most of the day, regardless of the weather.

The streets of Rome were quieter than usual, the soft patter of rain creating a peaceful atmosphere. As Clara made her way to the Vatican, she took in the beauty of the city, even under the gray skies. The ancient buildings looked majestic, their stone facades gleaming from the rain.

Upon reaching St. Peter's Square, Clara felt her heart race at the sight of the grand basilica. The sheer scale of the structure was awe-inspiring, its intricate details made even more beautiful by the raindrops clinging to the stone. She marveled at the statues of saints that adorned the colonnade, each one seeming to watch over the square with a sense of calm and authority.

Entering the basilica, Clara was immediately enveloped by the hushed reverence of the space. The interior was breathtaking—golden light streamed through the massive stained glass windows, casting colorful patterns on the marble floors. Clara felt a sense of peace wash over her as she walked down the central nave, taking in the grandeur around her.

One of the highlights of her visit was Michelangelo's Pietà, a stunning sculpture that captured the moment of Mary holding the lifeless body of Jesus. Clara stood in front of it, entranced by the emotion and craftsmanship. She had seen pictures of it before, but nothing compared to witnessing it in person. The sorrowful yet serene expression on Mary's face spoke volumes, and Clara felt a deep connection to the piece.

As she moved through the basilica, Clara encountered other visitors, some whispering in awe and others simply lost in their thoughts. She found herself thinking about her own journey, how she had come to Rome seeking adventure and inspiration, but had stumbled upon something much deeper—a sense of purpose.

After exploring the basilica, Clara ventured outside to the Vatican Museums. She joined a small group waiting in line, excitement bubbling within her. The rain had eased, leaving a cool, fresh breeze in its wake.

Inside the museums, Clara was greeted by a world of art and history. From ancient sculptures to Renaissance paintings, each room offered a new glimpse into the past. The highlights for her were the Raphael Rooms, where the brilliance of the artist's frescoes left her breathless. She lingered in the Room of the School of Athens, marveling at the depiction of philosophers in a grand architectural setting. It was as if the walls themselves were alive with intellectual discourse.

As she continued her exploration, Clara's mind wandered to Gianni. The connection they had forged felt so natural and exhilarating. She wondered what he would think of the art and history surrounding her. She hoped he would join her on future adventures, sharing in the experiences that made Rome so enchanting.

Clara's day was filled with wonder, but as she approached the end of her visit, she felt a hint of sadness. She wanted to capture every moment in her memory, to hold onto the magic of the day. She took photos, documenting her favorite pieces and the feelings they evoked.

Finally, she reached the Sistine Chapel. The line moved slowly, but Clara didn't mind the wait; she was eager to step into the sacred space that Michelangelo had transformed with his artistry.

As she entered, the atmosphere shifted. The silence was palpable, broken only by the hushed whispers of awe. Clara tilted her head back, her breath catching as she gazed at the breathtaking ceiling. The vibrant colors and intricate details told stories of creation, sin, and redemption. She felt as though she were witnessing a divine revelation, the weight of history pressing down on her in the best possible way.

Finding a quiet corner, Clara closed her eyes for a moment, allowing herself to absorb the energy of the chapel. She reflected on the journey she had taken to get to this moment—how her heart had been closed off after her breakup back home, yet now, with every new experience in Rome, it felt like it was slowly opening again.

After what felt like both an eternity and a fleeting moment, Clara reluctantly left the chapel, her heart full yet heavy. Outside, the sun peeked through the clouds, illuminating the Vatican in a warm glow. It felt like a blessing—a sign that the dark clouds of uncertainty were beginning to lift.

With her spirits lifted, Clara decided to make her way back to the apartment, her mind buzzing with thoughts. She felt compelled to share her experiences with Gianni, to recount the beauty she had witnessed. She could almost hear his laughter as he teased her about how she could spend an entire day in museums and still want more.

As she walked, she glanced at her phone, recalling their plans to meet later that evening. A sense of anticipation filled her at the thought of seeing him again. Clara found herself smiling, her heart racing at the prospect of their next adventure together.

Once back in her apartment, Clara took a moment to unwind, reflecting on the day. The combination of art, history, and the vibrant culture of Rome had rekindled a passion within her—a passion for exploration and connection. She felt more alive than she had in a long time, and it thrilled her.

As the clock neared 6 PM, Clara decided to freshen up. She chose a casual yet stylish outfit, hoping to impress Gianni without appearing overly dressed. After a quick makeup touch-up, she glanced at her reflection, feeling a rush of confidence.

When Clara arrived at their meeting spot, the sun was beginning to set, casting a warm orange hue over the buildings. She spotted Gianni leaning against a lamppost, his smile instantly lighting up her heart. "Hey! You look beautiful," he said, his eyes sparkling with genuine admiration.

"Thanks! I just came from the Vatican, and it was incredible," Clara replied, her excitement bubbling over.

"Did you see the Sistine Chapel?" he asked, his curiosity piqued.

"Yes! It was mind-blowing. I can't wait to tell you all about it," she said, her words flowing like the stories that had come alive in her mind.

As they strolled through the streets, Clara felt a deep connection to Gianni. They shared stories of their experiences in Rome, laughing and teasing each other as they ventured toward a local pizzeria for dinner. The aroma of fresh basil and baking bread filled the air, enveloping them in a sense of comfort.

Over dinner, they discussed their dreams for the future—traveling to new places, experiencing different cultures, and finding ways to connect with others. Clara felt a sense of warmth and openness with Gianni, realizing that this journey was not just about exploring the world but also about opening her heart to new possibilities.

As they finished their meal, Gianni suggested they take a walk to the nearby Tiber River. Clara eagerly agreed, her heart racing with anticipation. The night was alive with the sounds of laughter and music, and Clara felt like she was living in a dream.

At the riverbank, they paused, taking in the stunning view of the illuminated city. The reflection of the lights danced on the water, creating a magical ambiance. Clara turned to Gianni, her heart full, and said, "I'm so glad I came to Rome. It's not just the city that's beautiful; it's the experiences I'm having and the people I'm meeting."

Gianni smiled, his gaze holding hers. "I feel the same way. There's something special about this place, and I think it's even more special because I get to share it with you."

In that moment, Clara knew that this was just the beginning of a beautiful journey, one that intertwined their paths in ways she had never expected. With the Tiber River flowing beside them and the city of Rome sparkling in the night, Clara felt a sense of hope and excitement for what the future might hold.

11

Echoes of the Past

The following day, Clara awoke with a sense of wonder still lingering from the magical evening spent with Gianni. The sun filtered through her window, casting warm rays that danced across the walls. She smiled, recalling their laughter, the way their eyes met, and the promises of more adventures to come. Today was another opportunity to explore, and Clara felt a renewed sense of purpose.

After a quick breakfast, Clara decided to visit the ancient ruins of the Roman Forum. The sprawling site was a testament to Rome's grandeur and history, a place where echoes of the past whispered through the ruins. She took the short walk from her apartment, excitement building with each step as she approached the entrance.

Upon entering the Forum, Clara was enveloped by the grandeur of the ancient architecture. She wandered through the remnants of temples, basilicas, and public spaces, each stone telling a story of the civilization that once thrived here. Clara felt as though she had stepped back in time, imagining what life might have been like for the Romans who walked these paths centuries ago.

As she explored, Clara's imagination took flight. She pictured senators debating in the Curia, traders bustling in the marketplace, and families gathering in the temples to worship. The scent of history hung heavy in the air, and Clara found herself captivated by the beauty of the ruins, each fragment a piece of a larger puzzle.

She took her time, snapping photos and jotting down notes in her travel journal. Every corner offered a new perspective, a different angle from which to appreciate the architectural marvels around her. Clara felt a deep connection to the past, a reminder of the resilience and ingenuity of those who had come before her.

After hours of exploration, Clara found a quiet spot among the ruins, a small stone bench overlooking the Temple of Saturn. She took a moment to sit and reflect. Her thoughts drifted to Gianni. She wondered how he would react to the Forum, what stories he would spin about the ancient world. A part of her wished he were here to share the experience, but she knew that their paths would cross again soon.

As she sat there, a group of tourists gathered nearby, their guide animatedly explaining the history of the Forum. Clara listened intently, soaking in the information as she absorbed the atmosphere. The excitement of the guide brought the ruins to life, making Clara feel even more connected to the place.

After her break, Clara continued her exploration, eventually making her way to the Palatine Hill, one of the seven hills of Rome. The view from the top was breathtaking, offering a panoramic vista of the Forum and the Colosseum in the distance. She stood there, taking in the beauty of the city, her heart swelling with gratitude for the opportunity to experience such a remarkable place.

As the sun began its descent, casting a golden glow over the ancient structures, Clara decided to make her way to the Colosseum. The iconic amphitheater was on her must-see list, and she couldn't wait to stand before it. The excitement of the day and the energy of the ruins filled her with an insatiable desire to uncover more stories of the past.

Arriving at the Colosseum, Clara felt a wave of awe wash over her. The sheer scale of the structure was staggering, and she joined the line to enter, anticipation bubbling within her. Once inside, she marveled at the intricate design, imagining the roar of the crowd and the gladiators who once fought for their lives in the arena.

Clara wandered through the ancient corridors, the weight of history pressing in on her. She could almost hear the echoes of the past—the cheers of thousands, the clash of swords, and the gasps of spectators. The grandeur of the Colosseum was both exhilarating and sobering, a reminder of the dual nature of humanity—its capacity for entertainment and violence.

As she explored the lower levels, Clara felt a deep sense of respect for the lives that had been lost within these walls. The stories of bravery, despair, and triumph reverberated through the stone. Clara took a moment to sit on one of the worn benches, allowing herself to reflect on the experiences that had shaped Rome's history.

Lost in thought, Clara was startled when a familiar voice broke through her reverie. "Clara!" She turned to see Gianni standing a few feet away, his face lit up with a bright smile.

"Gianni! What a surprise!" Clara exclaimed, her heart racing at the sight of him. "I didn't expect to see you here!"

"I couldn't resist coming to see the Colosseum, especially after you mentioned it," he replied, stepping closer. "I'm glad I found you."

Clara felt a rush of warmth at his presence. "I was just soaking in the history of this place. It's incredible."

"I know! It's amazing to think about all the events that took place here," Gianni said, his eyes gleaming with excitement. "Want to explore together?"

"Absolutely!" Clara replied, her heart soaring.

As they wandered through the Colosseum together, Clara found herself reveling in Gianni's enthusiasm. He pointed out various features, sharing interesting facts about the amphitheater's construction and its role in ancient Roman society. They laughed and joked as they navigated the ancient corridors, each moment bringing them closer together.

After exploring the lower levels, they made their way to the upper tier. The view was breathtaking; Clara felt as if she were standing at the heart of Rome itself. With the sun setting in the distance, the city was bathed in a warm golden light, the shadows of the ancient ruins stretching across the landscape.

"This is incredible," Clara breathed, turning to Gianni. "I'm so glad you're here to share this with me."

"Me too," he said, his gaze steady on hers. "It's even better with someone who appreciates it as much as I do."

Clara felt a flutter in her chest at his words. There was something about Gianni that made her feel alive, as if the adventure was only just beginning. She realized that it wasn't just the sights of Rome that captivated her; it was the connection they were building, the laughter they shared, and the stories waiting to unfold.

As they stood together, looking out over the Colosseum and the sprawling city beyond, Clara felt a sense of contentment wash over her. She was no longer just a traveler in Rome; she was part of the narrative, weaving her own story among the echoes of the past. With Gianni by her side, she was ready to embrace whatever adventures awaited them in this timeless city.

With the sun dipping below the horizon, Clara knew this was just one chapter of many yet to come, and she was eager to see where the journey would lead.

12

A New Beginning

The next morning, Clara awoke with a sense of exhilaration coursing through her veins. After the incredible evening spent with Gianni at the Colosseum, she felt as if she was floating in a dream. The sun was just beginning to rise, casting soft hues of pink and orange across the sky, and Clara couldn't help but smile as she thought about the adventures that awaited her today.

She quickly showered and dressed, her heart racing with anticipation. Today was not just another day in Rome; it was the final day of her journey, and she wanted to make the most of it. With Gianni's enthusiastic spirit in her mind, Clara decided that she would take a different approach today—one that embraced spontaneity and the thrill of exploration.

After a hearty breakfast of pastries and espresso at a nearby café, Clara set off to meet Gianni at their agreed-upon location, the Trevi Fountain. The morning air was crisp, and the streets were filled with the lively chatter of locals and tourists alike. Clara took her time strolling through the vibrant streets, allowing the sights and sounds of Rome to envelop her like a warm embrace.

When she arrived at the Trevi Fountain, Clara was mesmerized by its beauty. The sun illuminated the cascading water, creating a shimmering effect that made the fountain seem almost magical. Gianni was already there, leaning against the fountain's edge with a charming grin on his face.

"Good morning, Clara!" he exclaimed, his eyes sparkling. "Ready for an adventure?"

"Absolutely!" she replied, feeling a thrill at the thought of exploring more of the city with him.

"First, let's toss a coin into the fountain," he said, pulling a euro coin from his pocket. "Legend says that if you toss a coin over your left shoulder with your right hand, you'll ensure a return to Rome."

Clara took a coin and followed Gianni's lead. They both closed their eyes and made wishes before tossing their coins into the fountain. As Clara watched the coins land in the water, she felt a wave of hope wash over her. She wished for new beginnings and cherished memories, a sentiment that resonated deeply with her recent experiences.

"Now that we've sealed our fate with the fountain, what's next?" Clara asked, her curiosity piqued.

Gianni leaned in, a mischievous smile spreading across his face. "How about we explore the Trastevere neighborhood? It's known for its charming streets, delicious food, and vibrant atmosphere."

Clara nodded eagerly. Trastevere was known for its narrow, winding streets lined with colorful buildings, and she had heard that it was a perfect place to experience the authentic spirit of Rome.

As they made their way to Trastevere, Clara felt a rush of excitement. Gianni's presence had a way of making everything seem more vibrant and alive. They navigated through the bustling streets, filled with the aroma of fresh bread and the sound of laughter from nearby cafes. Clara's heart swelled with joy as they immersed themselves in the lively atmosphere.

Once they reached Trastevere, Gianni led her down cobblestone streets that seemed to weave a tapestry of history and culture. They stumbled upon small artisan shops and local markets, where Clara marveled at handmade crafts and unique souvenirs. The sun filtered through the trees, casting dappled shadows on the ground, creating a picturesque backdrop for their adventure.

"Let's grab some gelato," Gianni suggested, pointing to a quaint gelateria. The thought of indulging in the creamy treat made Clara's mouth water. They ordered their favorite flavors—pistachio for Clara and stracciatella for Gianni—and settled at a nearby bench, enjoying the deliciousness while soaking in the vibrant atmosphere.

"Can you believe how much we've seen in just a few days?" Clara asked, savoring each bite of her gelato.

"It's incredible," Gianni replied, his eyes sparkling with enthusiasm. "But I have a feeling today will be the best yet."

After finishing their gelato, they continued to wander through Trastevere, discovering hidden gems around every corner. They visited the stunning Basilica di Santa Maria in Trastevere, admiring its beautiful mosaics that sparkled in the sunlight. Clara was captivated by the stories behind the artwork, which spoke of centuries of devotion and history.

As they explored, Clara and Gianni shared stories about their lives, dreams, and aspirations. With each revelation, their connection deepened, and Clara felt a sense of comfort and familiarity with Gianni that was rare for her. She realized how much she had grown in just a few days, and it was all thanks to the enchanting city and the unexpected bond they were forming.

With the sun beginning to set, casting a golden glow over the rooftops of Trastevere, Gianni suggested they head to Gianicolo Hill for a panoramic view of the city. Clara eagerly agreed, excited to see Rome from a new perspective.

The walk to Gianicolo Hill was steep, but Clara didn't mind. The anticipation of reaching the summit filled her with energy. As they climbed, they laughed and joked, their camaraderie making the journey feel effortless.

When they finally reached the top, Clara gasped at the breathtaking view. The entire city sprawled before them, with the iconic domes and rooftops creating a stunning landscape against the backdrop of the setting sun. The sky was painted in shades of orange, pink, and purple, casting a magical glow over the ancient city.

"Wow," Clara breathed, feeling as if she had stepped into a painting. "This is absolutely beautiful."

"Just like you," Gianni said softly, turning to look at her. Clara's heart raced at his words, and she felt a warmth spread through her.

"Thank you," she replied, her cheeks flushing. "This whole trip has been amazing."

As they stood there, taking in the beauty of Rome, Gianni reached for Clara's hand. The simple gesture sent butterflies fluttering in her stomach. She looked up at him, their eyes locking in a moment that felt charged with unspoken emotions.

"Clara, I know we haven't known each other long, but I feel a connection with you that I can't ignore," Gianni said, his voice earnest. "I want to see where this goes, if you're open to it."

Clara's heart raced at his admission. She felt the same way—a bond that transcended their brief time together. "I'd like that," she said softly, her voice barely above a whisper.

In that moment, surrounded by the beauty of Rome, they both understood that this was not just a fleeting encounter. It was the beginning of something special. As they stood there hand in hand, Clara felt the weight of her past lift and the promise of new beginnings blossom before her.

As the last rays of sunlight faded into twilight, they took a moment to simply enjoy each other's company, the city whispering secrets around them. Clara knew that while her time in Rome was coming to an end, the memories and connections she had forged would last a lifetime. With Gianni by her side, she felt ready to embrace whatever the future held, knowing that this chapter in her life was only the beginning of a beautiful story yet to unfold.

About the Author

Anny Winny is an emerging voice in contemporary African literature, known for her evocative storytelling and keen insight into cultural and social dynamics. Anny draws inspiration from her rich heritage and the everyday lives of the people around her. Her stories often explore themes of community, resilience, and the human spirit, offering readers a unique perspective on the complexities of rural and urban life in Africa.

With a background in education and a deep love for literature, Anny Winny's writing is both captivating and reflective, bridging the gap between traditional narratives and modern experiences. Her work is characterized by its authenticity and sensitivity, with characters who resonate deeply with readers. Through her stories, she seeks to spark conversations about unity, identity, and the importance of understanding diverse perspectives.

Anny Winny continues to write from her home, where she is actively involved in her community and dedicated to empowering young voices. "Ojukwu's Lapses" marks another significant contribution to African literature, showcasing her talent for weaving complex narratives that capture both the struggles and triumphs of her characters.

Milton Keynes UK
Ingram Content Group UK Ltd.
UKHW021927201124
451474UK00013B/968